PRAGUE
THE CITY AT A GLANCE

D1423668

Prague Castle
The city's pre-eminent landmark is a rambl.
affair of churches, palaces and presidential
offices. Proper exploration could take days.
Hradčanské náměstí, T 224 372 434

Trója Château
Elegant gardens front French architect Jean
Baptiste Mathey's baroque villa, built in the
late 17th century. It opens in the summer and
hosts a collection of historical Czech art.
See p096

St Nicholas Church
Kilián Ignác Dientzenhofer gave this church
its dazzling baroque interior in the first half
of the 18th century. Mozart played the organ.
Malostranské náměstí

Josefov
Bar several synagogues and an overcrowded
cemetery, little is left of the Jewish ghetto,
now a rather upmarket shopping district.

Charles Bridge
Saintly statues and cobblestones line Karlův
most, linking Malá Strana and Staré Město.

National Memorial
Extensive renovations have diminished the
lingering communist connotations but not
the powerful presence of this vast granite
complex that looms large in the east.
See p010

Tower Park
Constructed during the Soviet occupation, the
telecommunications tower is rumoured to
have been erected to jam Western broadcasts.
Artist David Černý's (see p061) surreal 2000
installation *Babies* clambers up the exterior.
See p013

INTRODUCTION
THE CHANGING FACE OF THE URBAN SCENE

It's hard to imagine now, but before the Velvet Revolution, Prague was a grey, rather mournful place to be – monumentally medieval, with cobbles and low-voltage street lighting underlining an Eastern Bloc backwardness. Then came the bright neon of capitalism. The changes were most noticeable in the post-revolution years, but the commercialisation has continued apace. Thankfully, in the centre, the burghers have kept development in check, except at Wenceslas Square, which has lost some of its art nouveau glamour; its slow transformation to a pedestrianised zone should restore some lost charm. Areas remaining untouched are also protected by a UNESCO World Heritage listing (and provide an ideal cinematic backdrop).

More recently, the annual Designblok festival celebrated its 20th birthday in 2018 and boasts more than 200 participants – testament to a burgeoning creative scene that is gathering speed. Since the late noughties, this has led to the launch of major galleries focusing on Czech and Slovak talent, such as DSC (see p060) and Dox (see p069), a multipurpose hub in Holešovice, a once off-piste district that has become one of the city's most exciting enclaves. At the same time, a new breed of entrepreneurs have localised bold concepts experienced abroad, and proprietors are realising that design does contribute to the bottom line. While much of Staré Město and Malá Strana can seem riddled with tourists and cheap Bohemian crystal, we will show you that Prague has a modern, sophisticated side too.

ESSENTIAL INFO
FACTS, FIGURES AND USEFUL ADDRESSES

TOURIST OFFICE
Prague City Tourism
Staroměstské náměstí 1
T 221 714 714
www.prague.eu

TRANSPORT
Airport transfer to city centre
Buses to metro line A depart from 4.23am
to 11.42pm, every three to five minutes at
peak times. The whole trip takes 35 minutes
www.prg.aero
Metro
T 296 191 817
www.dpp.cz
Trains run from 5am to midnight, and from
5am to 1am on Fridays and Saturdays
Taxis
AAA
T 222 333 222
It is advisable to book cabs in advance
Travel Card
Unlimited 72-hour travel on buses, trams,
metro and the funicular costs CZK310

EMERGENCY SERVICES
Emergencies
T 112
24-hour pharmacy
Lékárna Palackého
Palackého 5
T 224 946 982

EMBASSIES
British Embassy
Thunovská 14
T 257 402 111
www.gov.uk/world/czech-republic
US Embassy
Tržiště 15
T 257 022 000
cz.usembassy.gov

POSTAL SERVICES
Post office
Jindřišská 14
T 221 131 111
Shipping
UPS
T 233 003 300

BOOKS
Prague: An Architectural Guide by
Radomíra Sedláková (Arsenale Editrice)
**Prague, Capital of the Twentieth
Century: A Surrealist History** by Derek
Sayer (Princeton University Press)
Utz by Bruce Chatwin (Vintage Classics)

WEBSITES
Architecture
www.pragitecture.eu
Culture
www.goout.net
Newspaper
www.radio.cz

EVENTS
Designblok
www.designblok.cz
Signal Festival
www.signalfestival.com

COST OF LIVING
**Taxi from Václav Havel Airport
to the city centre**
CZK700
Cappuccino
CZK65
Packet of cigarettes
CZK95
Daily newspaper
CZK30
Bottle of champagne
CZK1,850

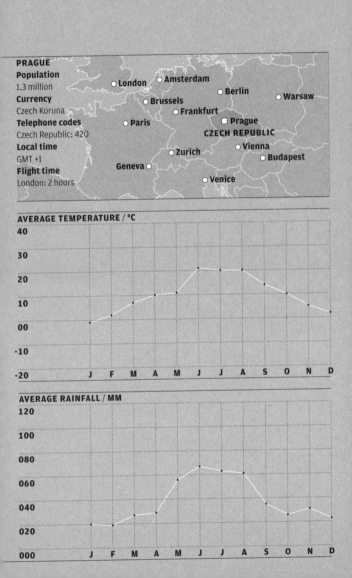

PRAGUE

Population
1.3 million

Currency
Czech Koruna

Telephone codes
Czech Republic: 420

Local time
GMT +1

Flight time
London: 2 hours

London · Amsterdam · Berlin · Warsaw · Brussels · Frankfurt · Prague · Paris · **CZECH REPUBLIC** · Zurich · Vienna · Budapest · Geneva · Venice

AVERAGE TEMPERATURE / °C

	J	F	M	A	M	J	J	A	S	O	N	D

40
30
20
10
00
-10
-20

AVERAGE RAINFALL / MM

	J	F	M	A	M	J	J	A	S	O	N	D

120
100
080
060
040
020
000

NEIGHBOURHOODS

THE AREAS YOU NEED TO KNOW AND WHY

To help you navigate the city, we've chosen the most interesting districts (see below and the map inside the back cover) and colour-coded our featured venues, according to their location; those venues that are outside these areas are not coloured.

HRADČANY

This rocky outcrop dominates the capital. It's the location of the Czech parliament and sprawling Prague Castle (see p009), whose extensive walls enclose palaces, a host of churches and a monastery. Visitors hustle for a place to watch the changing of the guard and to take in the mixture of architectural styles. On your way down, beat the crowds by using the less-trodden routes through beautiful hillside gardens.

NOVÉ MĚSTO/VYŠEHRAD

Between the strikingly modern extension of the neo-Renaissance National Theatre (see p073) and the art nouveau incline of Wenceslas Square lies the more consumer-oriented side of Prague. There are hordes of tourists, but you'll also see locals going about their everyday business. Frank Gehry and Vladimir Milunić's 'Dancing House' (see p014) is a highlight here, as is the craggy formation of Vyšehrad, home to the ruin of the city's less famous castle (see p009).

MALÁ STRANA

The apron of land below Prague Castle is a warren of narrow cobblestoned streets, and where you'll find embassies occupying baroque palaces, and luxe hotels, such as the Augustine (see p022) and the Mandarin Oriental (see p030). Parks and cafés like Cukrkávalimonáda (Lázeňská 7, T 257 225 396) dot the area leading to Charles Bridge. Overlooking it all is the Petřín Tower (see p009), built from railway tracks in 1891.

JOSEFOV

Discrimination against the Jews who lived here was reduced in part during the reign of emperor Josef II, after whom the area was named; synagogues surround the old cemetery. Rudolfinum concert hall (Alšovo nábřeží, T 227 059 227) is the most formal of the neighbourhood's many music venues. Chic shops cluster along Pařížská and in its environs: seek out Czech fashion at Vidda (Elisky Krásnohorské 134/9, T 739 333 444).

ŽIŽKOV/VINOHRADY

Separated from the historic centre by the unforgiving north-south *magistrála* (dual carriageway), these two boroughs provide an authentic taste of city life. Vinohrady is named for the vineyards that once covered this area, and its neo-Renaissance and art nouveau houses speak of previous wealth. The working-class neighbourhood Žižkov has a tougher feel. Take in the imposing National Memorial (see p010) and visit the retro space-age TV Tower (see p013).

STARÉ MĚSTO

A mishmash of lanes surrounds Old Town Square (Staroměstské náměstí), the site of the Town Hall's famous astronomical clock. This vast open area is a great spot to feast on some of Prague's 100 spires, particularly those atop the Disney-esque Týn Church (see p072). It's a full-on tourist trap, with pavement cafés and 'genuine' crystal, but classier venues like Le Valmont (see p044) provide some welcome respite nearby.

LANDMARKS

THE SHAPE OF THE CITY SKYLINE

There is no escaping history in Prague. Here, the most noticeable and impressive landmarks occupy the prime locations. Hradčany is, without doubt, where you'll find the king of them all – Prague Castle (Hradčanské náměstí, T 224 373 368). Enter the complex through the gates guarded by Ignác Platzer's ferocious baroque statues. To the south, Vyšehrad (V Pevnosti 159/5b, T 241 410 348), the city's secondary citadel, is less touristy and there's plenty to explore including an 11th-century rotunda. Between these two rocky outcrops, most of Prague lies on the plain of the Vltava River. City planners first overcame the problem of flooding by moving the street level up one floor. But the floods of 2002, which were the worst in centuries, were more troublesome. It took years, but new defence barriers were eventually completed.

Other key sights are often cheek by jowl and can be difficult to appreciate fully, particularly the buildings around Staroměstské náměstí (Old Town Square), which range from the Romanesque and Gothic, like Týn Church (see p072), to the rococo. However, the absence of modern high-rises does mean that the older parts of the city preserve their charm. For a superlative overview, head up the 63.5m Petřín Tower (Petřínské sady, T 257 320 112). From here, you can pick out the two modernist insertions of Tower Park (see p013) and the colossal National Memorial (overleaf) across the river. *For full addresses, see Resources.*

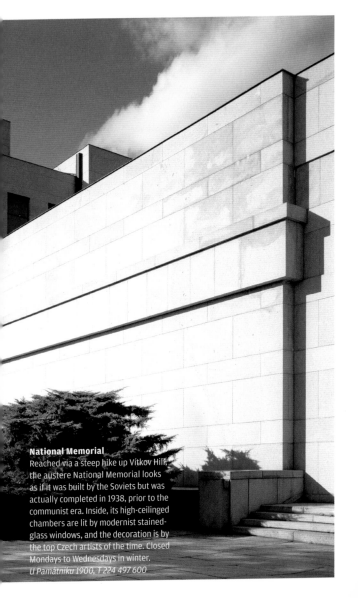

National Memorial
Reached via a steep hike up Vítkov Hill, the austere National Memorial looks as if it was built by the Soviets but was actually completed in 1938, prior to the communist era. Inside, its high-ceilinged chambers are lit by modernist stained-glass windows, and the decoration is by the top Czech artists of the time. Closed Mondays to Wednesdays in winter.
U Památníku 1900, T 224 497 600

Stroj Času

From 1955 to 1962, this site in Letná Park bore an enormous statue of Josef Stalin leading four burly proletarians, known colloquially as '*Fronta na maso*' ('The line for meat'), a wry reference to the regular food shortages under communism. It was the largest sculpture in Europe until it was destroyed after Khrushchev's denunciation of Stalin, blown up in a series of explosions that went on for months. In 1991, Vratislav

Karel Novák's kinetic artwork *Stroj Času* ('Time Machine'), a symbolic reference to the passing of the years and the changing of regimes, was installed on the plinth. The 25m-high painted steel metronome beats about three times per minute, although it is not always working. It can be spotted from much of Old Town and overlooks the 1908 art nouveau Svatopluk Čech Bridge. *Letná Park*

Tower Park

Formerly called the Žižkov TV Tower, this 216m spike typifies the often outlandish creations of the communist era, although it took seven years to construct and wasn't finished until after the revolution, in 1992. Three silver columns support the rocket-like edifice. Attempts have been made to liven up its greyness, from David Černý's *Babies* to the coloured under-lighting of the platforms. In 2012, Atelier SAD gave the bistro and bar a retro-futuristic feel and added a luxury hotel suite. From the enclosed lookout deck 93m up, you can enjoy a 360-degree view of Prague while suspended in Eero Aarnio 'Bubble Chairs'. In fair weather, the National Memorial (see p010) and statue of the medieval general Jan Žižka somehow appear within reach. *Mahlerovy sady 1, T 210 320 081, www.towerpark.cz*

Nationale-Nederlanden Building

Dubbed the 'Dancing House', this striking piece of statement architecture, designed by Frank Gehry, of course, in collaboration with Vladimir Milunić of Studio VM, gets additional exposure thanks to its location right next to the river. As is often the case with contemporary interventions of such visual drama, the 1996 building has as many detractors as fans. Gehry's remarks that he deliberately pinched it in at the waist so that neighbours' views would not be spoilt were greeted with scepticism by those who believe that it is little more than an advert for his unfettered ambition, at the expense of this historic city. The good news is that a trip to make up your own mind is made worthwhile by a visit to the seventh-floor restaurant Ginger & Fred (T 221 984 160): a meal here comes with some outstanding panoramas thrown in.
Jiráskovo náměstí 1981/6

HOTELS

WHERE TO STAY AND WHICH ROOMS TO BOOK

Hotels continue to open in Prague, and the resultant oversupply represents good news for visitors on two fronts. Firstly, pricing is very competitive, and secondly, savvy operators have been busy refurbishing their existing establishments to compete. An example is the Four Seasons (Veleslavínova 2a/1098, T 221 427 000), which provides fine views across the river, and has kept up to speed with makeovers by Pierre-Yves Rochon. Other stalwarts have changed hands and been relaunched. In 2019 the Charles Square became a Radisson Blu (Žitná 561/8, T 225 999 999), set in an 1898 building, and the W (Václavské náměstí 826/25), which arrived here in 2020, is a revamp of the art nouveau Grand Hotel Europa. The Mandarin Oriental (see p030) is another headline act, incorporated into a site that dates from the 14th century, and the sceney Buddha-Bar Hotel (Jakubská 649/8, T 221 776 300) caters to a party crowd.

Hotel Josef (see p023) was the city's first design property when it opened in 2002, and was followed by a range of hi-tech, modern accommodation. A new wave of independent offerings with real personality stand out, notably The Emblem (see p019) and The Emerald (see p020), while Miss Sophie's (Melounova 3, T 210 011 200) is a cheery boutique choice with a bijou spa in its brick vaults, and Port X (V Přístavu 4, T 606 724 138) is a contemporary houseboat with wraparound windows for four people moored in Holešovice. *For full addresses and room rates, see Resources.*

Carlo IV

This landmark near the Old Town makes a striking architectural statement. The drama starts in the lobby, formerly a banking hall (although the building became the Czech post office HQ under communism), where gilt and marble abound. Restaurant guru Adam D Tihany designed the Inn Ox Lounge and adjacent backlit bar, while the original pillars throughout the property are draped in organza-like steel curtaining. Many of the rooms, however, tend to veer towards the chintzy; we would suggest opting for the relatively elegant Junior Suite, which has an art nouveau vibe. Two of the hotel's most popular features are the 20m mosaic-tiled pool under the arches in the basement (above) and the wood-panelled speakeasy in the vault, which specialises in cognac. *Senovážné náměstí 13/991, T 224 593 111, www.dahotels.com/carlo-iv-prague*

Boho Hotel

Barcelona firm GCA bought and converted this 1911 commercial building into a rare contemporary hotel for Prague, behind an art nouveau exterior with painted wood panelling. For its 2015 launch, extra floors were added to two of the three 'wings' to make it a homogenous five storeys and an interior courtyard was reborn, into which a glass-box restaurant was inserted (there are complimentary wine tastings for guests here). Elsewhere, there's a library (above), a basement spa with an enticingly lit sauna and jacuzzi, and a lounge facing the street with a line of fluted pendant lights above a pulpis stone bar. The 57 rooms continue the palette of dark brown, blue, grey and ochre, with black metal fixtures, and have high ceilings and arty photos of the city. *Senovázná 1254/4, T 234 622 600, www.hotelbohoprague.com*

The Emblem

Bang in the centre of town, The Emblem was carved out of a stately 1908 apartment block in 2013. Designer Alison McNeil has combined original pieces, such as a sinuous sofa by Vladimir Kagan, with custom-made furnishings, from the white-glass 'Potato Lamps' by Bartosz Swiniarski illuminating the corridors to the sconces by sculptor Carmen Salazar. The rooms feature walnut desks, brass lamps and Elitis' textured linen wallpaper. Opt for the Suite Library (above), which feels like a cosy pied-à-terre, with an attic bedroom and a copper tub by William Holland. A growing art collection includes local illustrators Tomski&Polanski's tribute to their city, *The Monument*, spread across five floors. Hit George Prime Steak (T 226 202 599) for aged beef and rare bourbon. *Platnéřská 111/19, T 226 202 500, www.emblemprague.com*

The Emerald

Inside a 1906 period building, The Emerald is the vision of Frenchman Pierre Emmanuel Dionnet, who runs Urbanium Concept. The 16 unique residences are richly layered in textures and materials, poetically themed and cinematically styled. The largest, the two-bedroom, two-bathroom Iwa (above and opposite), is pure wabi-sabi. It features plenty of weathered wood, slate details and a monochrome palette of white, black and shades of grey, notably in Tomáš Magrot's patinated walls, and two custom pieces by local artist Aleš Novák, including a painted spruce panel by the freestanding tub. On booking, you are sent a code to access the property and pick up the key. There's daily housekeeping, but no common facilities, although there is plenty on the doorstep. *Žatecká 17/7, T 602 666 982, www.the-emerald-prague.com*

Augustine

Fashioned around seven buildings, one of which dates back to the 13th century, this hotel takes its name from the adjacent Augustine monastery. Interiors by Olga Polizzi and London-based RDD reflect the monastic theme – as do the treatments in the spa (T 266 112 273), which also has a hammam – with a pared-down decor that mixes local references like cubist-inspired furniture, wrought-iron and glass. The best key is for the Presidential Suite (above), which offers a spacious living room, a four-poster bed and a bathroom with heated marble floor. The bar has a high baroque ceiling decorated with frescoes of angels; in summer the service extends to the lovely cloisters and garden. Try the St Thomas beer, which was first brewed here in 1352. *Letenská 12/33, T 266 112 233, www.augustinehotel.com*

Hotel Josef

She may be based in London, but Czech-born architect Eva Jiřičná has a soft spot for her Prague hotel project, the Josef, which she designed inside and out. The all-white lobby features her spiralling glass staircase, and the 109 bedrooms are divided between two blocks, the Pink and Orange Houses, which are linked by an emerald lawn where guests can enjoy breakfast during the summer. Glassed-in bathrooms in most of the accommodations help to counteract their relatively compact dimensions. Some, like Room 801 (above), have a balcony and offer appealing views of Prague Castle. Josef's central location means it's well situated for dining out: the Michelin-starred La Degustation Bohême Bourgeoise (T 222 311 234) is nearby.
Rybná 20, T 221 700 901,
www.hoteljosef.com

24 HOURS

SEE THE BEST OF THE CITY IN JUST ONE DAY

Prague is a wonderful city to amble around, aside from the cobbles, perhaps. Out of season, nothing beats getting lost in Staré Město or idling by the river, on Kampa Island (see p068), or the Náplavka embankment (see p074), a hip hangout with floating galleries and bars. To put your feet up, hop on a tram (Route 22 is a good tour). And the metro is worth a trip, if only for the ultra-steep escalators (Náměstí Míru has the longest in the EU) and the platform walls, in particular of Line A, which opened in 1978; artist Jaroslav Votruba encapsulated stop-motion travel with coloured rows of anodised aluminium tiles in repetitive convex and concave patterns.

Have a liquid lunch at T-Anker (Náměstí Republiky 656/8, T 722 445 474) on top of the 1975 Kotva department store, a honeycomb of communist-era brutalism designed by Vladimír Machonin and Věra Machoninová. Local brewery Matuška, and Permon in Sokolov supply the pumps, but it's all about the views, from the gargoyles on the art nouveau Hotel Paris to the baroque towers poking over the rooftops. Dinner tends to be taken early, around 7.30pm. To sample Czech fare, head to Field (see p031) or Zdeněk Pohlreich's Next Door (Zlatnická 3, T 295 563 440) for dishes like deer with elderberry sauce and sautéed *spaetzle* with juniper. Then follow the crowd to a beer hall (see p050) such as Pivovarský Klub (Křižíkova 17, T 222 315 777) or, in the summer, the beer stands in Letná park. *For full addresses, see Resources.*

09.00 Phill's Corner

The once rundown district of Holešovice, a mix of residential blocks and warehouses, is developing nicely thanks to an art scene centred around DOX (see p069) and the Holport design centre, which launched in 2000 within a former metalworks. The 1911 building is home to the Konsepti furniture flagship, various interiors brands and Phill's Corner, which comprises a café, a deli and a store proffering design goods. The slick space is the handiwork of Jan Plecháč and Henry Wielgus (see p065); Lasvit (T 222 362 990), which is also based here, made the geometric lighting installation. Come for breakfast – third-wave coffee and thick toast topped with fried eggs, crème fraiche and chives. If you are visiting later in the day, Phill's Twenty7 (T 605 444 528), owner Filip Mičan's hip bistro, is round the corner. *Komunardů 32, T 731 836 988*

10.30 Veletržní Palác

Oldřich Tyl and Josef Fuchs' Trade Fair Palace was one of the first functionalist buildings in Europe. Completed in 1928, it occupies an entire block, and formerly housed offices, a cinema, restaurants and an observation deck. After 1951, it was an HQ for foreign-trade companies until a fire in 1974 reduced it to a skeleton. It finally reopened in 1995 as a wing of the National Gallery, displaying modern and contemporary Czech and European art. Rotating exhibitions have included Alfons Mucha's *Slav Epic*, a series of 20 monumental canvases, and Franz West's *Epiphanien* sculptures (above). Also look out for paintings by local masters Jakub Schikaneder and František Kupka. Refuel at on-site Café Jedna (T 778 440 877). *Dukelských hrdinů 47, T 224 301 122, www.ngprague.cz*

12.30 House at the Black Madonna

In the years preceding WWI, an exclusively Czech architectural style was developed in the reconstruction of Josefov. Cubism uses pyramids, triangles and prisms to produce sculpted facades and surfaces in diamond-cut or crystal-like forms. The House at the Black Madonna, named after the baroque edifice it replaced (the statue was moved to its facade), designed by Josef Gočár and constructed between 1911 and 1912, is one of the best examples. It houses the Grand Café Orient (T 224 224 240), where you can take lunch, and Kubista Gallery (see p094). Also check out Josef Chochol's 1913 Triplex House (Rašínovo nábřeží 42/6) and Otakar Novotný's Teachers' Cooperative (Elišky Krásnohorské 7), a final cubist flourish in 1919. Its pink palette is an amusing contrast to the muscular torsos of the telamones. *Ovocný trh 19*

15.00 Galerie Jaroslava Fragnera

One of the only museums in the country dedicated to architecture and the applied arts is set in a Gothic-era building that dates back 600 years. Across two storeys it displays often-provocative exhibitions, such as 'Spaces of Desire' (above), a rather off-the-wall exploration of architecture and sexuality, and presents the work of local and global practices. Affectionately dubbed Fragnerka, it is named after the architect who studied with Josef Gočár (see p027), and would later design the House of Culture in Ostrava. The gallery here was established while Fragner was working on a rebuild of the neighbouring Bethlehem Chapel (T 224 248 595) in the early 1950s – and it is well worth also taking a peek at this atypical work.
Betlémské náměstí 5a, T 222 222 157, www.gjf.cz

17.00 Artisème

Behind the 'Lennon Wall', a counterculture protest site since the 1960s graffiti-tagged with messages of love, peace, democracy and freedom, Czech design store Artisème opened in 2018 in a beautiful setting in the *sala terrena* of a baroque palace with an 800-year history. Through the portal is a surprisingly large garden with an ancient sycamore (the story goes that Beethoven sat beneath it in the 18th century), where launches, fashion shows and other events are held in summer. Local firm Andrea a Martina custom-made fittings to meld with the stone floors and a gorgeous, vaulted frescoed room. On sale are glass, ceramics, jewellery and furniture from classic studios such as Milan Pekař and Dechem, as well as emerging talent like Eliška Monsportová. *Velkopřevorské náměstí 4, T 776 493 169, www.artiseme.com*

18.30 The Spa at Mandarin Oriental

Just entering The Spa at Mandarin Oriental is a rather divine experience, set as it is in an overhauled Renaissance chapel. The lobby (above) is situated in what was once the nave, and the altar of a Gothic church, uncovered during the excavation of the site, is displayed beneath thick glass floor tiles. London-based designer Khuan Chew carved out seven treatment rooms, decorated in darkwood and marble. For a therapy with a local touch, try the Linden Embrace, which includes a body scrub and massage with linden poultices (the tree is a Czech national emblem). There's also a mineral pool and steam shower. Afterwards, treat yourself to *kulajda* (mushroom) soup, a Prague favourite, and nasi goreng at the hotel restaurant Spices (T 233 088 777). *Nebovidská 459/1, T 233 088 655, www.mandarinoriental.com/prague*

20.30 Field

This casual, low-key restaurant surprised many by grabbing a Michelin star – one of only three in Prague at the time – in 2016, a year after it opened. Fans of chef Radek Kašpárek's rich, umami-focused cuisine, however, knew that the secret was out. The menu promises 'free-range dining', and there's a touch of New Nordic foraging to it, backed up by the classic fare of central Europe: rabbit, lamb, veal and game, as well as stone fruits, forest berries and root vegetables. There's a strong Czech angle, from an excellent riesling by cult producer Dobrá Vinice to cheeses from Krasolesí dairy in the Vysočina highlands. The sleek interiors are by Atelier Ph5, and feature an illuminated installation by Jakub Matuška and a scythe motif by Studio Najbrt.
U Milosrdných 12, T 222 316 999,
www.fieldrestaurant.cz

URBAN LIFE

CAFÉS, RESTAURANTS, BARS AND NIGHTCLUBS

The Czech Republic is the true home of *pivo* (lager). Staropramen is still made here in the capital, or try pilsners from Plzeň, including Urquell and Gambrinus. Local hostelries tend towards the Bavarian vernacular – open halls with communal tables as at U Zlatého Tygra (Husova 17, T 222 221 111) – and beers arrive without you ordering them, as there is an assumption you'll continue drinking. However, designer micro-breweries such as Dva Kohouti (Sokolovská 81/55, T 604 611 001) and Ossegg (Římská 45, T 603 264 390) have added sophistication. Alternatives are also more comprehensive – head to Veltlin (Křižíkova 488/115, T 725 535 395) for natural wines, and Hemingway (Karolíny Světlé 26, T 773 974 764) and Black Angel's (Staroměstské náměstí 29, T 224 213 807) for original cocktails. There are stylish third-wave coffee options as well, notably Kávarna Místo (Bubenečská 12, T 727 914 535) and Mazelab (see p037).

The culinary scene has refined too, typified by the contemporary interpretations of classic staples served in bistros The Eatery (see p036) and Eska (see p047). Meanwhile, the choices of cuisine are diversifying. The city's sizeable Vietnamese community now has a trailblazing fine-diner in Taro (Nádražní 300/100, T 777 446 007), while Manifesto (Na Florenci 23, T 702 048 247; March to December) is an open-air gourmet market in retooled shipping containers, with global and Czech food stalls, film screenings, bands and DJs. *For full addresses, see Resources.*

Kro Kitchen

This diminutive rotisserie (the kitchen takes up a third of the room) opened in 2019 on the lively square surrounding Jože Plečnik's church (see p079) and the farmers' market here provides Kro with many ingredients. Founder/chef Vojtěch Václavík's experience in Scandinavia is clear – the kimchi is made in house, for instance. The specialities are roast chicken, prepared with an umami-like dry rub of fermented onion and chilli with a herb and spice base, and pulled pork knuckle, marinaded in Prague powder, brine and sugar, and smoked and baked, served with sides and sauces such as plum XO. To drink, there's beer and natural wine. Local studio Neuhäusl Hunal's interior – plywood furniture, subway tiles, a checked floor – is tied together by a bespoke zigzag light. *Vinohradská 1013/66, T 721 030 017, www.krokitchen.cz*

Kuchyň

Next to Prague Castle, located inside what was very likely the kitchen of the 1811 Salm Palace, this is a celebration of traditional home-cooking. There's no menu here. After the day's soup, left on tables in a porcelain tureen, or a starter, you're invited up to the centrepiece stove adorned in cerulean tiles, where the lids of massive copper pots are lifted for you to choose with your senses. Chef Marek Janouch takes inspiration from historic recipes of the nobility, some in a 16th-century cookbook, to offer six mains. Beef in red wine, and pork schnitzel fried in lard and then roasted are always available; others, such as rabbit in mustard sauce, are seasonal. The house Kozel beer (unfiltered, black) comes from a tank. The candle-esque pendant lights are by Olgoj Chorchoj, and textile art is by Štěpánková & Kladošová. In summer, there are 120 seats on the terrace. *Hradčanské náměstí 2, T 736 152 891, www.kuchyn.ambi.cz*

The Eatery

There are no flowers or art for decoration at The Eatery. Just a strikingly simple concrete scheme by Neuhäusl Hunal, with handcast 'Kalla' pendants by Loftlight above the 25 tables, and an open white-tiled kitchen with counter seating. Chef Pavel Býček opened his upscale bistro in 2018 in Holešovice to offer classic Czech cuisine made with locally sourced seasonal ingredients (meat from revered butcher Martin Klouda, fish from Kalendova Chabrybárna, vegetables from family farms), brought bang up to date. For example, for the *vepřové v mrkvi*, the pork is confit overnight, grilled over charcoal and presented with three preparations of carrot and a braising sauce. In the evening, lights from the wine store shine through a cinder-block screen, adding to the cosy ambience.
U Uranie 954/18, T 603 945 236, www.theeatery.cz

Mazelab Coffee

A hyper-minimal daytime coffee hangout launched by designer/barista Jackie Tran in 2019, Mazelab is one of the first signs of gentrification in Dejvice. Located in an old car repair shop, the all-white backdrop of the spacious, low-ceilinged, skylit interior hits you first, as artificial light reflects off the walls, floor and perforated counters, on which sits a custom-made Kees van der Westen Spirit espresso machine and batch-brew pourers in black. Dotted around are retro stools and tables, school chairs and makeshift seating on breezeblocks, cheese plants, banana trees and strelitzias. The simple menu is stencilled on the wall, and drinks come in Japanese-style cups on trays with a card listing provenance, strength and so on. Note there's no sugar, wi-fi or cash.
Československé armády 26,
www.mazelab.coffee

Moon Club

In a former bank converted in 2019 by local firms Formafatal and Machar & Teichman, this dapper club revolves around a curved bar under a glass atrium, resplendent with a multicoloured bottle installation and a dangling forest of pendant lights. To the sides are a small dancefloor and seating nooks with edge-lit circular mirrors and velvet sofas and chairs, while upstairs is a lounge serving sushi and tapas, and VIP areas bedecked with patinaed metal sheets, burned wood and ornamental paintings. DJs play R&B, Latin, funk and reggaeton, often accompanied by a violinist or saxophonist and dancers, and the crowd is usually over 30 and smart. Open Tuesday to Saturday, until 4am at the weekends — arrive before midnight or book a table to ensure entry.
Dlouhá 709/26, T 703 140 640,
www.moonclub.cz

SmetanaQ Café & Bistro

On the riverbank, SmetanaQ is a design and art hub in a renovated 1847 property. Local firm Qarta uncovered century-old paint but otherwise the shell has been left raw aside from Preciosa chandeliers and huge 'Tim' pendants by Olgoj Chorchoj for Bomma. The Café & Bistro, decorated with oak parquet and Kateřina Handlová's 'Shibari' lighting inspired by Japanese bondage, is pleasant for breakfast (avocado eggs benedict, etc) or lunch (salads, burgers, pasta, waffles); coffee is by local roaster Doubleshot and brews by Tea Mountain in Karlín. Opposite, Deelive (T 222 263 526) offers a superlative overview of Czech creativity, from ceramics to glassware, fashion and jewellery by up to 50 makers. Up the stairs are many of their studios, and a gallery for art exhibitions. *Smetanovo nábřeží 334/4, T 722 409 757, www.smetanaq.cz*

Kavárna Co Hledá Jméno

This long-shuttered woodworkers emerged as the 'Café in Search of a Name' in 2016. Chestnut trees shade vintage chairs and tables in the backyard, while the interior combines the long communal tables of a co-working space with boho elements, like mismatched armchairs, and a hefty willow trunk that functions as a counter (above). Choose from espresso, Chemex, drip and Aeropress options, using arabica from native micro-roaster Nordbeans, or try the house-made lemonade, Prague microbrews or a ginger G&T. Art is on show throughout, and a separate gallery space puts on exhibits by local talent. The area is still nascent, but the vegan restaurant Pastva (T 736 115 336) and noodle bar Prolog (T 775 005 007) are worth a visit.
Stroupežnického 493/10, T 775 466 330, www.kavarnacohledajmeno.cz

Dvojka
Created by Jan and Henry (see p065), this
funky wine bar envisioned by gallerist/
owner Richard Preisler is awash in white
paint, even splattered over the floor to
resemble a studio. The intimate spot fits
a maximum of 25 people, who invariably
get to influence the soundtrack. Try the
Kosík chardonnay, or the orange varietal
from Halm, along with some local paté.
Veletržní 302/40, T 603 416 248

Le Valmont

This underground lounge/club takes its inspiration from nightspot Raspoutine in Paris, and the Czech film director Miloš Forman's *Valmont*. It has a genuine feel, due to its setting in early 14th-century stone arches, and touches like the house special, Le Gin Occulte, produced by cult distiller Martin Žufánek; staff dresses by designer Tatiana Kovaříková; and crystal chandeliers from Bohemian glassworks firm Preciosa, teamed with custom-made Aubusson carpets. The bespoke cocktails compete for attention with Czech wines and French champagnes. There's a strict dress code and room for only about 100 revellers in an intimate space consisting of several smallish rooms across various levels, including a dancefloor in the cellar. *Uhelný trh 414/9, T 601 141 134, www.levalmont.cz*

Bistro Proti Proudu

In a 1930s building, this café, whose name translates as 'Against the Current', has an inspired design by local firm Modulora in partnership with atelier Mimosa. From a perforated plywood wall, parallel lines of black cables stretch up from individual switches, configured in the same pattern as the tables, and spread over the ceiling to every pendant light to form a graphic installation. The rest is kept simple, with oak furniture, marble floors and a Corten counter. Journalists Karolina and David Konečni's bistro is popular with new-media types, who network over great coffee and all-day breakfast, or colourful dishes like pea pesto crostini with pecorino and fried egg. Desserts, such as mango purée panna cotta with edible flowers, are exquisite.
Březinova 471/22, T 728 036 171,
www.bistroprotiproudu.cz

Art Restaurant Mánes

On the site of the Šítkovské mill straddling a tributary of the river (the original tower dates to the 16th century), the 1930 Mánes Association of Fine Artists was a hangout of famous figures including Antonín Slavícek, Alfons Mucha and Mikoláš Aleš. In 2015, it was renovated into a refined restaurant by Michal Postránecký, who chose a palette of cream and brown to limit distraction from the views through floor-to-ceiling windows.

It is renowned for Jaroslav Zahálka's super Czech and French cuisine – paprika chicken breast, beef *bourguignon* with celery mash, *české buchty* (sweet buns) in rum-infused custard – and its expansive terrace, but it also functions as a gallery. There are pieces by Jiří Straka and Martin Lukáč, and ceiling frescoes by cubist painter Emil Filla. *Masarykovo nábřeží 250/1, T 730 150 772, www.manesrestaurant.cz*

Eska

A downstairs café and bakery by day and an upstairs restaurant by night, which reworks traditional recipes using influences from New Nordic and other culinary movements, Eska provides a refreshing change from the pork-heavy focus of local fare. Vegetables take a star turn in dishes such as a salad of heirloom tomatoes in house-made vinegar, smoked fish comes with potatoes in ash, dried egg yolk and the kitchen's own kefir,

and there is a daily eight-course seasonal tasting menu. Other fermentations create unorthodox beverages, like plum juice with a *tibicos* culture. It's set in a former factory with a high roof, skylights and steel girders. The interior decoration rotates every three or four months – one previous installation featured video projections of forest scenes.
Pernerova 49, T 731 140 884,
www.eska.ambi.cz

Bokovka

The original incarnation of Bokovka (which translates as 'Sideways' and is a tribute to the film) was a semi-private wine club. In 2015 it went public, albeit in a small cellar hidden away in a courtyard. Tricked out by architect Tereza Froňková, its rough walls of peeling plaster, flickering candles, cosy alcoves, melted-wax-and-fluorescent-tube chandeliers by Jiří Černický and projected silent black-and-white films combine for a seductive atmosphere. It is helmed by a quartet of sommeliers. Their selection is strictly European, with roughly a third from the Czech Republic (from producers such as Stapleton & Springer, Jaroslav Osička, Jakub Novák, Jaromír Gala and Ota Ševčík), and around 20 bottles are available by the glass. At the entrance, salami, sardines and cheese are prepped in a makeshift kitchen.
Dlouhá 37, T 731 492 046, www.bokovka.com

Vinohradský Pivovar

Prague has some excellent cocktail bars, like Bonvivant's CTC (T 775 331 862) and L'Fleur (T 734 255 665), but the preferred after-work drink has always been beer. In 2014, this stylish microbrewery opened within the cellars of the former Vinohrady Burghers Brewery, dating back to 1893. It swiftly became a go-to spot for excellent traditional *světlý ležák* (pale lager) and a slightly sweeter amber lager, as well as newer craft styles, such as IPAs. Architects OV-A retained the original vaulted arches, and large porthole windows in the stone walls display the fermentation tanks. The menu lists beer-hall dishes, like schnitzel with potatoes. Co-founder František Richter now runs two other brewpubs, including Pivovar u Bulovky (T 602 431 077) in Libeň. *Korunní 2506/106, T 222 760 080, www.vinohradskypivovar.cz*

Meetfactory

Named after its original home in a former Holešovice butcher, Meetfactory relocated to this enormous 1920s glassworks after the premises were devastated by the 2002 floods. It reopened in 2007 as a cluster of studios and performance spaces, and now operates the largest artist-in-residence programme in the country, as well as a 150-seat theatre, which puts on experimental performances, and a 750-capacity music hall. Visual arts, primarily from emerging local talent, including Kateřina Šedá and Václav Magid, are shown in two galleries and on the facade of the building (above), which has an installation by David Černý (see p061). The café/bar is open every day, serving coffee and speciality beers, and an in-house club puts on ad-hoc gigs. *Ke Sklárně 3213/15, T 251 551 796, www.meetfactory.cz*

Nejen Bistro

One of Prague's hardest-hit areas during the 2002 floods, blue-collar Karlín is now on the rise, its industrial heritage being commandeered by cultural spaces, design showrooms and hip publishing houses, as wine bars, boutiques and restaurants also move in. Nejen ('Not Only') Bistro's design, by local firm Mar.s Architects, melds oak floors, whitewashed brick, monochrome patchwork tiling and clustered lightbulb 'chandeliers'; it sets a calm vibe despite the bustle. In the milder months, sidewalk tables with park views alleviate the crush. Ingredients from nearby farms anchor the rotating menu, in dishes such as beetroot carpaccio, or meats cooked on the Josper grill. On tap are rare draft lagers from the small Moravian producer Pivovar Dalešice. *Křižíkova 24, T 721 249 494, www.nejenbistro.cz*

Jazz Dock

Architect Pavel Suchý's punchy interiors in this long-running gig venue incorporate a candy colour scheme offset by an acid-yellow 'futuristic-cubistic' bar front made of reflective laminate. Specialist acoustic interventions reflect the importance of the music to the owner, Vladimír Lederer, who, along with his partner, Karla Fišerová, was inspired to create an affordable club that would bring jazz back to the people of Prague. The single-storey construction appears to float as if moored on a narrow side channel of the Vltava but, in fact, as its name implies, it is grounded on the bank, allowing for a deck overhanging the water. The roster features up-and-coming talents and famous names; there are usually two concerts per night, at 7pm and 10pm. *Janáčkovo nábřeží 2, T 774 058 838, www.jazzdock.cz*

INSIDER'S GUIDE

LENKA MÍKOVÁ, ARCHITECT

'It is a magical city, full of stories, hidden corners and unexpected views,' says Lenka Míková of her hometown. The architect lives by the river near two of her favourite buildings, Emauzy Monastery (Vyšehradská 49/320), with its 1960s spires, and CAMP (see p066). She often has lunch in 'hip' Letná, at Bar Cobra (Milady Horákové 688/8, T 777 355 876), or drops into the 'cute courtyard garden' at Super Tramp Coffee (Opatovická 160/18, T 777 446 022) and slick patisserie Cukrář Skála (V Celnici 1034/6, T 220 199 381). On days off, she'll catch exhibitions at Dox (see p069), Galerie Rudolfinum (Alšovo nábřeží 12, T 227 059 205) or Kvalitář (Senovážné náměstí 1628/17, T 739 003 582): 'It focuses on the intersection of art, design, architecture and science.' And for retail therapy, her advice is to visit workshops such as Backyard (see p080), or the 'amazing studio – an oasis' of jeweller Janja Prokíc (Uhelný trh 414/9, T 774 374 312).

A fan of Asian fusion, she loves Taro (see p032), 'for the whole experience', and homely Sansho (Petrská 25, T 739 592 336): 'Its soft-shell crab slider is legendary.' Afterwards, she might head for wine at Bokovka (see p048), cocktails at Martinez (Budečská 773/19, T 702 123 040), a gig at Jazz Dock (see p053) or, 'when I prefer beats to bed, club Ankali (Lopuchová 58) has a great sound and ambience'. She adds: 'To feel the essence of Prague, go to Charles Bridge at 4am. You might happen to be there alone, in the fog, or under the stars.' *For full addresses, see Resources.*

ART AND DESIGN
GALLERIES, STUDIOS AND PUBLIC SPACES

'We are living in the Left Bank of the 1990s,' declared the *Prague Post* in 1991, as David Černý (see p061) exploded onto the scene. But the hangover from communism lasted 25 years longer than expected. Under leading lights Bohumil Kubišta, František Kupka and Alfons Mucha, the First Republic had been remarkably sophisticated, but creativity was publicly suppressed under totalitarianism. Yet many artists remained active during this era and their work is now being rediscovered, inspiring today's scene – Veletržní Palace (see p026) displays a fine overview. Meanwhile, since Hunt Kastner (see p062) opened in 2005, Žižkov has developed ad hoc into an arts district; check out experimental venues like City Surfer Office (Bořivojova 67, T 606 381 616), 35m2 (Víta Nejedlého 23, T 777 589 954) and Nevan Contempo (U Rajské zahrady 14, T 605 969 618).

The plastic arts have a storied history. Glass production began in the 15th century in the forests of Bohemia, which yielded the raw materials, and porcelain has been manufactured since the 18th century. Formed in 1885, the Prague School of Decorative Arts – now AAAD (see p065) – produced a stream of artisans from the 1920s, as well as luminaries such as the minimalist František Vízner, in whose hands glass was an artform. Contemporary makers remain innovative (see p083); seek out pieces in Praguekabinet (Platnéřská 13, T 212 241 410), Qubus (see p087) and Cihelna (see p090). *For full addresses, see Resources.*

Prague House of Photography

One of seven key venues encompassed by Prague City Gallery, including the Municipal Library (see p064), the PHP's roots stretch back to 1989, when its main aim was to find spaces to stage photography exhibitions. It wouldn't have its own until 2010, when the institution moved into a 1937 seven-storey block by German architect Fritz Lehmann, distinctive for the decorative arches in its stone facade that reach up to the first floor and are offset by circular openings. Its two storeys present primarily Czech talent in three annual shows. Past highlights have included the surreal portraiture of Pavel Baňka, and works by Lukáš Jasanský and Martin Polák, who shot a series of images of busts by Polish sculptor Alfons Karny to explore post-socialist themes in 'J/P/K'. *Revoluční 1006/5, T 702 283 922, www.ghmp.cz*

Galerie SPZ

Image-maker Lukáš Machalický and paper/ acrylic artist Robert Šalanda launched this anything-goes gallery in a former garage in 2011. The automotive vibe lives on – SPZ stands for *státní poznávací značka* (licence plate), which is the reference point for the brand identity. It presents a programme of experimental and confrontational art. Past shows have featured Czech talent such as abstract painter Tomáš Predka, film-maker Adéla Babanová and installation specialist Filip Dvořák, as well as international names like Swedish sculptor and illustrator Jonas Nobel. 'Do you Jump Queues?' (above) was a cross-section of exhibitions and activities here over five years, including interviews with the creatives. Every three months, SPZ commissions a design for a large-format flag, which is hung over the entrance.
Pštrossova 8, www.galeriespz.com

Lucie Drdova Gallery

After stints in museums and galleries in Berlin and Vienna, Lucie Drdová opened her own venture in Žižkov in 2012, and it quickly became one of the beachheads for a blossoming scene. She represents a group of prominent Czech artists, as well as Slovaks and Slovenians permanently resident here, including photography duo Hynek Alt and Aleksandra Vajd, painters Daniel Vlček and Monika Žáková and the conceptual sculptor and video artist Pavla Sceranková. The programme also includes other Prague-based artists such as Václav Magid ('Anti-Nature vs Anti-Culture vs Anti-Future', above) in two rooms with polished resin floors and windows onto the street. Drdová is a co-author of the useful English-language *Czech Contemporary Art Guide*. *Křížkovského 1288/10, T 777 216 416, www.drdovagallery.com*

DSC Gallery

Rudolf Netík, the architect responsible for the design of DSC, knows a thing or two about display. His work for many of the stores on Prague's upscale shopping avenue Pařížská, including Versace and Ermenegildo Zegna, testifies to this. In 2009 he brought Olga Trčková and Petr Šec's idea for an art venue to life nearby, installing his signature cut-outs in the floor, which both catch the attention of passersby on the street, and open up the space. DSC champions Czech and Slovak artists, including glass legend Václav Cigler, as well as Ašot Haas, Jiří Černický, Jakub Matuška (aka Masker), Roman Týc, Milan Houser and Prague painter Martin Krajc ('Welcome to Paradise', above). Open 1pm to 7pm except Sunday, or by appointment. *Dlouhá 923/5, T 607 262 617, www.dscgallery.com*

Kafka Sculpture

David Černý became a household name when he painted a Soviet tank memorial pink in 1991. Acerbic, supersized pieces by the enfant terrible are now all over the city, often in unexpected corners, but never subtle. His *Babies* crawl up Tower Park (see p013), while a statue of St Wenceslas sits comically on a strung-up dead horse inside Palác Lucerna (T 224 224 537). The kinetic bust of Franz Kafka was installed in 2014 on the 90th anniversary of the novelist's death. It comprises 42 layers of stainless steel that rotate independently: the face disassembles and reassembles, and is perfectly aligned roughly every 10 seconds. It is entitled *K.*, after the tragic hero of *The Trial*, Josef K., whose attempts to grasp what he has been accused of by an inscrutable court are foiled at every turn. *Charvátova/Vladislavova*

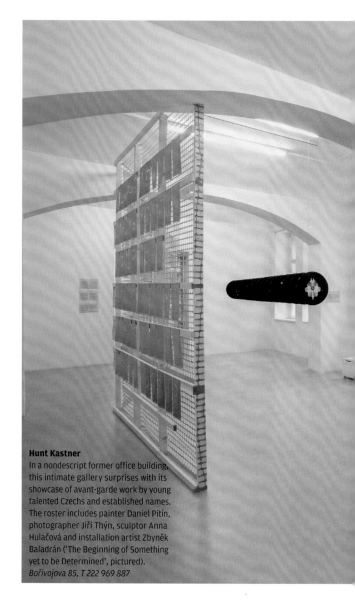

Hunt Kastner
In a nondescript former office building, this intimate gallery surprises with its showcase of avant-garde work by young talented Czechs and established names. The roster includes painter Daniel Pitín, photographer Jiří Thýn, sculptor Anna Hulačová and installation artist Zbyněk Baladrán ('The Beginning of Something yet to be Determined', pictured).
Bořivojova 85, T 222 969 887

Municipal Library of Prague

Prague's central library was conceived as a cultural institution. Built between 1925 and 1928, the grand municipal structure boasts a travertine facade, and was designed by František Roith, a student of Otto Wagner. Above the main entrance sit six allegorical sculptures by Ladislav Kofránek, and inside there's a central hall with an ornamental ceiling decorated in geometric patterns by František Kysela. The exhibition spaces on the second floor were acquired in 1992 by Prague City Gallery (see p057). Broadly covering neo-constructivism, minimalism and geometry, here you'll catch shows that feature artists such as postwar painter Jan Merta, cross-media maverick Petr Nikl, and Václav Cigler and Michal Motyčka, who are known for their light installations (above).
Mariánské náměstí 98/1, T 222 310 489, www.mlp.cz

Jan Plecháč & Henry Wielgus

These two AAAD graduates established their studio in 2011 following a commission from Cappellini, who saw Plecháč's degree show and asked the duo to produce a piece for its Milan exhibition. The result was the 'Circle' chair, with a geometric body made of overlapping rings of red steel-wire. The pair have since designed lighting for Lasvit, and interiors (see p025), plus playful, eco-conscious furniture, such as the corrugated 'Ondulé' tables and mirror, available from Harddecore (T 775 417 230). Created for London gallery Mint, the 'To Be Concrete' mirror (above) has a diameter of 80cm but is only 1cm thick. It sits on a powder-coated metal stem, and its height can be adjusted on a five-point scale. The base of concrete discs is inspired by the weights that are used to keep overhead railway lines taut. *T 604 475 144, www.plechacwielgus.com*

CAMP
The 2017 Center for Architecture and Metropolitan Planning (CAMP) presents planned city projects and exhibitions on the urban environment, often interactive, in a large hall with a 25m projection wall on the ground floor of Karel Prager's 1973 brutalist classic. It also hosts screenings, a slick café and an outpost of art/design bookstore Pagefive (see p080).
Vyšehradská 51, T 770 141 547

Museum Kampa

Meda Mládek befriended Czech painter František Kupka in Paris in the 1950s, and went on to acquire more than 200 of his works, followed by collages and objects by Jiří Kolář. Her collection expanded in the 1960s following visits to artists' studios in Poland, Hungary and Yugoslavia, and with a series of sculptures by Otto Gutfreund. When she donated it all to Prague, the city decided to house it in an historic mill on Kampa Island. In the rebuild, Viennese architect Helena Bukovanská kept a few elements of the dilapidated structure, like the gable and tower, and added steel and glass walkways in a partly deconstructed facade crowned by an 'exploding' cube. Rotating exhibitions ('7+1 Masters of Czech Glass', above) also take over the courtyard. *U Sovových mlýnů 503/2, T 257 286 147, www.museumkampa.cz*

Dox

This pioneering centre was a catalyst in the gentrification of Holešovice. Founded in 2008 by Leoš Válka, it is one of the few independent Czech art institutions, and set out its stall in 2009 with David Černý's controversial *Entropa*. It still shows edgy works, and addresses social issues, while occasionally revisiting past masters – a retrospective on sculptor Karel Nepraš was followed by a reconstruction of his *Family Ready for Departure*. Local architects Ivan Kroupa transformed a cluster of industrial buildings into a spacious complex linked by polished concrete ramps and staircases. In 2016, Leoš Válka and Martin Rajniš' wood-and-steel 'zeppelin' literary salon landed on top, and in 2018, Petr Hájek's extension for performing arts was nominated for a Mies van der Rohe Award. Closed Tuesdays. *Poupětova 1, T 295 568 123, www.dox.cz*

Hrabalova Zeď

Czech novelist Bohumil Hrabal, a master of poetic expressionism, is revered in his homeland but not so well known overseas (read *I Served The King Of England*). After his death in 1997, the city commissioned this tribute in his old stomping ground of Libeň. The 'Hrabal Wall', a mural by the local painter Tatiana Svatošová-Cipárová, depicts the man himself, his beloved cats and Perkeo typewriter, as well as some of his texts, painted at the site of his home, which was torn down during construction of the subway. To find it, take the B line to Palmovka station and go up the escalators in the direction you were travelling, exit left and then turn right. Street art aficionados should also check out Pasta Oner's cartoon slogans and the colour-saturated shapes (often distorted circles) by Jan Kaláb.
Na Hrázi 326/24

ARCHITOUR

A GUIDE TO PRAGUE'S ICONIC BUILDINGS

The centre is a mesh of historic styles: the Romanesque crypts under St Vitus Cathedral (Pražský hrad III nádvoří 48/2), the Gothic spires of Týn Church (Celetná 5, T 222 318 186), the Renaissance Queen Anne's Summer Palace at Prague Castle (see p009), and many striking baroque and rococo buildings. In the early 20th century, art nouveau and Secessionist movements took hold, followed by cubist and other modernist influences. Fine examples are Adolf Loos' Villa Müller (see p077) and the 1932 Villa Palička (Na Babě 9), Mart Stam's input to the Werkbund's Baba housing estate.

After the communist takeover in 1948, creativity suffered. The concrete-panelled swathes of suburban housing are best seen from a distance, and many state buildings and hotel towers are faceless. However, the era did see the addition of a few laudable structures such as the former Parkhotel Praha (Veletržní 1502/20, T 225 117 111), a 1967 modernist slab by Zdeněk Edel, Tower Park (see p013), Nová Scéna (opposite) and the old Federal Assembly of Czechoslovakia (see p076). After the Velvet Revolution, any potential development was restricted by the UNESCO World Heritage listing in 1992 that declared that Prague had 'influenced the development of perhaps all European architecture'. As for what the future holds, given the furore surrounding the late Jan Kaplický's green-and-purple 'blob' proposal for the National Library, it may not be quite so exciting. *For full addresses, see Resources.*

Nová Scéna

To celebrate the centenary of the National Theatre, the epitome of neo-Renaissance drama inaugurated in 1883, local architect Karel Prager dreamt up this extraordinary addition, which squares up to the original across Divadelní. Nová Scéna (New Stage) has plenty of presence of its own – it is a 25m-tall bevelled rectangle clad in more than 4,300 blown-glass blocks designed by Czech artist Stanislav Libenský – and is best viewed at sunset when the facade is aglow. Its 400-seat auditorium hosts opera, ballet and performing arts. But you don't need to buy a ticket to view the magnificent interior (see p055), which is clad in Verde Serrano marble. A sculptural chandelier by Pavel Hlava and Jaroslav Štursa hangs from the ceiling right down through the stairwell. *Národní 4, T 224 901 448,*
www.narodni-divadlo.cz

Náplavka

Since the millennium, the 3km of attractive riverbank south of the Dancing House (see p014) has been evolving into a cultural hub thanks mainly to architect Petr Janda. He spearheaded the arrival of (A)void Floating Gallery, also a bar and event space (T 602 211 181), cyclists' café Bajkazyl (T 739 681 839), the Forman brothers' theatre ship Tajemství (T 777 261 338) and a farmers' market. His firm Brainwork has now hewn 19 further premises from former storage set into the embankment's massive stone walls. Clad in grey plaster with glossy metal fittings, they were unveiled in 2020. Six on the eastern side have 5m circular porthole-style 'lenses' (they are the largest elliptical pivoting windows in the world, nicknamed 'Prague's Eyes') that rotate diagonally and serve as entrances. They host community ventures including a DIY repair café, a zero-waste coffeeshop and a municipal library branch, as well as ateliers and art spaces.

National Museum New Building

This hybrid encapsulates Prague's modern history better than the collection it holds. Jaroslav Rössler's 1938 stark stone stock exchange (above, back left), a muscular symbol of capitalism, was commandeered by the communists in 1946. Karel Prager's extension, from 1966 to 1974, went above and beyond, quite literally – a horizontal Vierendeel-truss steel giant with sinister tinted windows that cantilevers over the top on pillars. It was purposefully brutal, to challenge the pretty opera and National Museum on either side, and this, coupled with its function, has ensured an enduring unpopularity, despite hosting Radio Free Europe for 14 years. For Prager, however, it was an exemplar of a spatial concept to combat urban sprawl, to build houses over houses, and ultimately cities over cities. *Vinohradská 1, T 224 497 430*

Villa Müller

The culmination of Adolf Loos' Raumplan conceptualisation of residential spaces, Villa Müller was finished in 1930. A spiral plan of rooms is set around a staircase. Cubist elements can be seen throughout: in the plum-and-velvet-upholstered sofa placed between two marble blocks; the radiator cover in the Japanese-inspired summer room; and the planters on the roof. From the green-grey Cipollino de Saillon marble used to clad the walls of the main hall to the mahogany of the dining-room table and its coffered ceiling, the quality of the materials shines through. Loos rated the villa as his best work. It was fully restored in 2000. Book in advance to take a tour, which run every two hours on Tuesday, Thursday, Saturday and Sunday. *Nad hradním vodojemem 14/642, T 224 312 012, www.muzeumprahy.cz/mullerova-vila*

Church of St Wenceslas

Along with the eventual completion of the 14th-century St Vitus (see p072) and the imposing 1932 Church of the Sacred Heart (Jiřího z Poděbrad náměstí), designed by Slovenian Jože Plečnik, this was the third project commissioned for the millennium of Prague's patron saint in 1929, and the most progressive. Josef Gočár was known for his cubist style (see p027), but here, in Vršovice, he embraced functionalism in sharp, white concrete, and tackled the sloping terrain with a 'staircase' roof that ascends in four glazed steps towards the apse, which has a stained-glass window by Josef Kaplický (Jan's father) and sculpture by Čeněk Vosmík. Above an inviting open foyer, a slender belltower rises 50m and is topped by a 7m cross, yet the building slots beautifully into its suburban surroundings.
Svatopluka Čecha náměstí, T 702 075 417

SHOPS

THE BEST RETAIL THERAPY AND WHAT TO BUY

There's more to shopping here than the stores lining Pařížská, which include Cartier (No 2) and Rolex (No 14), as well as local jewellers Halada (Pařížská 1076/7, T 724 986 111). Nearby Dlouhá and its side streets are an enclave of indigenous creativity, exemplified by the womenswear designers Klára Nademlýnská (Dlouhá 3, T 224 818 769) and Timoure et Group (V Kolkovně 6, T 222 327 358). Indeed, ladies are well catered for – seek out DNB (Náprstkova 4, T 222 221 342) and Leeda (Bartolomějská 304/1, T 775 601 185) by the river. There are collective showrooms too, with in-house workshops and studios where you can meet the makers – drop into Backyard (U Obecního dvora 2, T 605 894 096) and Deelive (see p040).

Outside the centre, the shops get quirkier. Tiny Bohemian Retro (Chvalova 8, T 607 914 992) is crammed with dresses, accessories, glassware and other heirlooms. In Vinohrady, Nila (Korunní 91, T 777 755 837) purveys organic cosmetics and homewares. Over the river, Papírna (Františka Křížka, T 252 547 452) proffers joyful stationery made from recycled paper, and bookshop and publisher Pagefive (Veverkova 5, T 735 852 693) promotes young Czech artists, sells original prints and celebrates all forms of visual culture. Treat your drinks cabinet to a bottle of absinthe from Martin Žufánek, which also produces quirky gins and little-known regional spirits such as kontušovka, available at Bartida (Havelská 500/25, T 224 281 247). *For full addresses, see Resources.*

Hana Zárubová

Works-in-progress and incompleteness are repeating themes in Hana Zárubová's futuristic yet timeless fashion. The concept also provided inspiration for her second-floor showroom inside a 1926 functionalist building, a collaboration with set designer Henrich Boráros. Walls appear as if about to be painted, floors are cracked, lighting is bare, wiring is exposed, grey felt seating looks like concrete slabs and scaffolding poles hung on cables act as rails. Known for voluminous coats and interactive pieces (the polyester 'Arrange Windbreaker' can morph from short to long, and from casual to sophisticated), Zárubová uses materials including wool combined with neoprene and memory-effect lightweight polyamide. There is also a fledgling menswear line. *Biskupský dvůr 1147/6, T 727 818 566, www.hanazarubova.cz*

Luciela Taschen

Slovak designer Lucia Jamrichová works with Czech artisans to create beautifully crafted handmade bags. They are defined almost by their simplicity – no zippers, no lining, subtle metal details – and modern shapes. The LT Basics collection is made in rich-coloured leather, but she has also incorporated materials including Piñatex for the LT Vegan range (such as the flat, U-shaped 'Plochá Tasche', which has an integrated handle), cork and even upcycled art exhibition banners. For the cute store, Formafatal devised a modular grid of rebar rods to display the wares on top of peeling plaster and paint, and lattice-like prints by Eva Hanzalová. In this retail enclave, also visit Hana Zárubová (see p081), Showroom (see p086) and Lavmi (T 230 234 976). *Petrská 1135/10, T 777 873 447, www.lucielataschen.com*

Atelier Pelcl

The world's first glass factory was founded around 1414 in Chřibská (it only closed in 2012, six centuries later), and by the 18th century, Czech crystal was being exported globally. Continuing this impressive legacy, a new coterie of companies that includes Lasvit, Bomma, Brokis and Verreum have been producing the work of today's talent, notably Rony Plesl, Jan Plecháč & Henry Wielgus (see p065), Olgoj Chorchoj and Atelier Pelcl. Founder of postmodern group Atika in the late 1980s, Jiří Pelcl designed Václav Havel's study in Prague Castle and directed the AAAD, where he still teaches. His glass pieces, like the architectural 'GEO' vase (above), are functional yet dynamic; find select items in Designum (T 257 317 960). He says: 'I create objects that evoke emotions, that are tactile, almost sensual.' *www.pelcl.cz*

100Class Concept Store
Located in on-the-up Petrská, Vendula
Stoklásková's boutique, set inside a
townhouse, features a rotating edit of
clothing, accessories and homewares
from native makers, including fashion
designer Hana Zárubová (see p081)
and jewellers Alžběta Dvořáková and
Jana Voňková. There are also European
cult brands, like Langackerhäusl bags.
Soukenická 1096/30, T 604 833 822

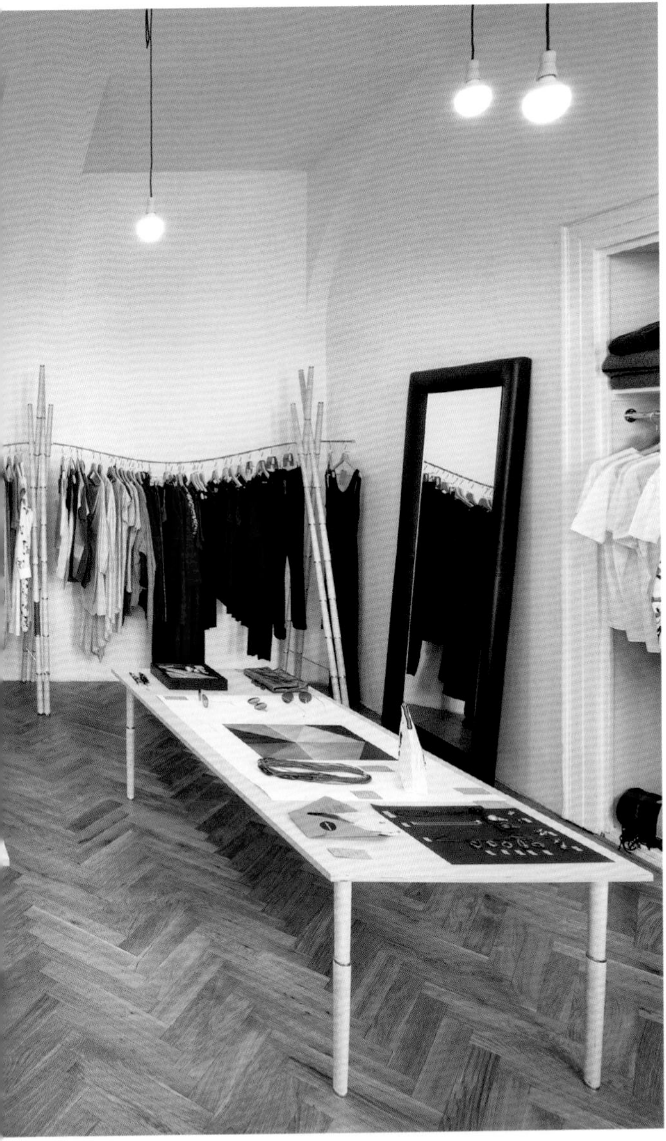

Showroom

Head to the hip Petrská quarter to discover a select group of fashion designers, many of whom work here on site. Owner Zuzana Hartlová trained as an architect, and her own line, Soolista, displays a strong sense of shape in deconstructed shirts and coats made primarily from natural fibres, often with little embellishment and a raw finish that emphasises the qualities of the fabric. Co-founder Klára Šípková creates jewellery from laser-cut stainless steel, and more unusual materials. You'll also find leather accessories by Two Lines and handmade shoes by Dyan from Hungary. The bijou store has a monochrome scheme, and a clever black-steel framework device that links rails and tables, holding the space together under high 19th-century ceilings. *Klimentská 3, T 605 047 771, www.showroomdot.cz*

Qubus Design Gallery

The first design gallery in Prague, Qubus was launched in 2002 by Jakub Berdych and Maxim Velčovský with a focus on their own studio's production, all of it handmade in Bohemia. Its glassware and ceramics often have a surreal element – the 'Hände Hoch' candlestick gives the impression that fingers are burning, and Velčovský's porcelain vases are sculpted as a pair of Wellingtons, covered with Moravian folk motifs. Today, Berdych runs the show on his own, in addition to a spacious store in the Dox (see p069) complex. There you'll find architectural jewellery by Eva Eisler, traditional wooden toys by the legendary Ladislav Sutnar, and glass items ranging from František Vízner reproductions to pieces by today's leading makers such as Dechem and young gun František Jungvirt. *Rámová 3, T 222 313 151, www.qubus.cz*

Naše Maso

Reviving the revered traditions of Czech butchery, 'Our Meat' dry-ages its steaks for up to 50 days, stuffs its own *salsiccia* and *talián* sausages, and boasts the best take on Lower East Side pastrami in this corner of Europe. The fleckvieh beef and Přeštice pork comes direct from local farms, and then there's the Prague ham, of course. Naše Maso will grill anything from the counter for takeout, including the city's favourite hamburger and a mean mustard hot dog, served in bread baked in nearby Čelákovice. If you want to sit down, there's a reservation-only 'butcher's table' menu from Monday to Wednesday after 7pm. Also for sale are sauces, oils, spices and broths. Note that there are many other delis located along this 'gourmet passage', from wine to chocolate and cheese shops. *Dlouhá 39, T 222 311 378, www.nasemaso.cz*

Chatty

Czech fashion designers Radka Sirková and Anna Tušková's womenswear label has gained a tribe of followers and high-profile clients since its inception in 2005. Garments are progressive, sharply tailored and structural, and feature leather, denim and silk. The showroom, which opened in 2012, functions as both a workspace and a boutique. The brainchild of architect Jiří Zhoř of Studio Muon, also behind the cute Mistral Café (T 222 317 737), it has a pared-back, industrial vibe that mirrors the sartorial concept of muted tones and texture, using steel, oak beams and raw concrete panels. As well as ready-to-wear, there's a bespoke denim service, offering full customisation, a choice of more than 25 types of fabric and a lifetime warranty. *Haštalská 21, T 608 139 967, www.chatty.cz*

Cihelna

Situated in a former brickworks, inside a pleasant courtyard, this chic concept store/gallery with interiors by Michaela Tomišková showcases contemporary Czech glassware, porcelain, jewellery, lighting and furniture. You might find pieces by Mária Čulenová, Studio Revír or Adéla Fejtková, as well as the local English-language design 'zine *Soffa*. *Cihelná 2b, www.cihelnaprague.com*

Antipearle

Photographer and jeweller Markéta Dlouhá Márová set out to give the classic pearl a (chic) punk edge. Her first piece, in 2008, the 'Fang Up' ring, a large freshwater pearl flanked by two upturned curving spikes in sterling silver, was inspired by a shark's tooth, and is now an icon of the cult label. She spends part of the year in the Azores where she dives and returns to the surface with ideas, including for the interior of her riverfront boutique, devised with local artist Michal Cimala. It evokes a fantasy seascape via otherworldly sculptures that function as displays. Her output may have softened but it still packs in plenty of attitude, such as the 'Sirene Pearl Earcuff', which resembles a monster, and the statement 'Megalodon' pendant and 'Jaws' or 'Crescent' necklaces. *Janáčkovo nábřeží 61, T 703 333 206, www.antipearle.com*

Debut Gallery

The ancient arches of this concept store, adjacent to the Old Town square, are set off by a minimalist interior. Within, many of the most interesting pieces on display are jewellery, chosen by owner Kateřina Rezková, such as the fine silver rings and necklaces made by Janja Prokić, and gold earrings festooned with freshwater pearls that resemble peony flowers from Zorya. Look out for Milan Pekař's ceramics, in particular his porcelain vases that have crystalline glazes in vibrant, contrasting hues – the bright colours are created in part by temperature adjustments during firing. Local fashion includes slipper-style shoes from Cutulum; garments for women by Hana Zárubová (see p081); and smart unisex accessories from Pavel Brejcha. *Malé náměstí 12, T 602 600 058, www.debutgallery.cz*

Kubista Gallery

Pablo Picasso and Georges Braque's cubist movement that begun in Paris in 1907 soon took hold in Prague, due to painters Emil Filla and Bohumil Kubišta. More uniquely, it later manifested itself in applied arts and architecture, thanks to an avant-garde group that included Pavel Janák, Vlastislav Hofman, Josef Gočár and Josef Chochol, until the onset of WWI. Post-independence, there has been renewed interest in this national style. Kubista Gallery, founded in 2002 to showcase cubist (and post-1925 art deco) design, is set in Gočár's House at the Black Madonna (see p027). Originals, such as Janák's 1911 ceramic hand-painted coffee pot (above), CZK3,790, are displayed alongside replica items and contemporary pieces inspired by the movement.

Ovocný trh 19, T 224 236 378, www.kubista.cz

Book Therapy

On a quiet street in Vinohrady, in a 1903 art nouveau building painted mint green and adorned with its creator's name (Karel Horák) in gold letters, Book Therapy lives up to its name. It's owned by Petra Caudr Hanzlíková and Jiří Caudr, who run craft-focused design store Lípa (T 728 459 699) in the centre. On offer is an impressive edit of art, design, fashion and culture titles in English – we picked up local architecture magazine *Intro*. Prague studio Vobouch, known for its work with concrete, subtly incorporated it throughout – on cabinets, wrapped around the desk and in bespoke light fittings – along with salvaged-wood tables. You can book an evening's browsing for two people, with Moravian wine or tea from Momoichi (T 721 364 002) next door. *Římská 35, T 223 009 949, www.booktherapy.cz*

ESCAPES

WHERE TO GO IF YOU WANT TO LEAVE TOWN

Prague's popularity means the centre chokes with tourists, to say nothing of the oppressive summer heat. Instant escape is provided by the water bowsers that patrol Wenceslas Square spraying a fine mist, ostensibly to damp down dust. More breathing space can be found a few kilometres north on the Vltava's banks. Trója Château (U Trojského zámku 1, T 283 851 614) is a bold pink baroque villa fronted by a handsome garden. The interior decor of murals and marquetry provides the backdrop for a collection of Czech art.

Once you have made it past the frankly dull suburbs, you soon reach the rolling green landscape of Bohemia. Between the woods, fields of hops line the hills – this is beer country, after all – and Plzeň, the home of pilsner, is just over an hour's drive south-west. Take a tour of Plzeňský Prazdroj brewery (U Prazdroje 64/7, T 377 062 888). En route, stop at the dramatic, fairytale-esque Karlštejn Castle (Beroun, T 311 681 617), with its Gothic panels and murals. Also to the west are the spa towns of Karlovy Vary, famous for its 19th-century architecture, and the quieter Mariánské Lázně (aka Marienbad). To the south, medieval Český Krumlov is unarguably charming. Further east, two hours or so from the capital, the second city of Brno is worth a visit for Villa Tugendhat (see p098) alone, its significance assured when it was chosen as the location for the signing of the 1992 agreement to dissolve Czechoslovakia.

For full addresses, see Resources.

Entrée Restaurant, Olomouc

Just over two hours by train from Prague, Olomouc's well-preserved Old Town could rival the capital's – and it doesn't have the crowds. Head to Horní náměstí to view the Holy Trinity Column, a 35m-tall monument built from 1716 to 1754 by locals in gratitude for surviving the 1713 plague, and the 15th-century Town Hall and astrological clock. Stay at the Theatre Hotel (T 585 312 441), part of a Corten-clad complex by Atelier-r that encompasses a wellness centre and Entrée Restaurant, with nature-inspired interiors by Komplits Studio. The chef's table (above), illuminated by plant-filled Bocci pendant lights, is an invitation into the open kitchen. Přemek Forejt's tasting menu encompasses courses such as wild boar with hispi, juniper and raisins.

Ostravská 1, T 585 312 440,
www.entree-restaurant.cz

Villa Tugendhat, Brno

Grete and Fritz Tugendhat asked Mies van der Rohe to design their superlative three-storey home, and it has echoes of his 1929 German Pavilion. Completed a year later, Villa Tugendhat also features strong horizontal planes, despite sloping terrain, floor-to-ceiling windows and an open-plan layout – interrupted only by a semicircular cubby of Macassar ebony and a statement wall of white-veined honey onyx (pictured). With Lilly Reich, Van der Rohe also created the original furniture, including the 'Tugendhat' and 'Brno' chairs, often using tubular steel. The family fled to Switzerland in 1938 and the villa was trashed in the war. It later functioned as a dance school and a hospital. In 2012, it was restored to mint condition and is now open to the public. *Černopolní 45, T 515 511 015*

Hotel Ještěd, Liberec

Perfectly accentuating the mountaintop contours, the 'Czech building of the 20th century' (people's vote) is straight out of *The Jetsons*. Karel Hubáček and engineer Zdeněk Patrman's design incorporated a hotel and TV transmitter in one. It needed special cladding to protect against the cold and prevent interference, and a pendulum to absorb sway – a technological triumph considering it was constructed from 1966 to 1973, under communism. Otakar Binar's funky interiors still define the observation bar/restaurant, the circular corridors with his hanging egg chairs (above) and some of the rooms. In summer, hike to the Frýdlant and Sychrov castles, and in winter, there are ski trails and well-kept pistes. It's two-and-a-half hours on the train to Liberec, and then a cable-car ride to the summit. *Horní Hanychov 153, T 485 104 291*

Mezi Plůtky, Moravia

In converting a 200-year-old smelt-house director's cottage into a four-suite retreat, architect-designer Daniela Hradilová has balanced the old and the new. The classic shingled roof, ceiling beams, oak doors, pine window frames and sandstone floors are offset by Karl Andersson & Söner chairs, Hay bar stools, a 'Rocking Sheep' by Povl Kjer and a wool tapestry based on artwork by Petr Nikl. In the garden is a swimming pond and two wood barns, one for winter with a huge fireplace and dining table, the other a summer retreat, and furniture by Ronan & Erwan Bouroullec. It nestles in the Beskid mountains, a four-hour drive east of Prague. Take a day trip to the pretty town of Štramberk to sample its 'ears' (gingerbread rolls said to have been baked to celebrate the 1241 defeat of the Mongol invaders, who had cut off ears as military trophies). *Čeladná 266, T 606 924 232, www.meziplutky.cz*

NOTES
SKETCHES AND MEMOS

RESOURCES
CITY GUIDE DIRECTORY

A

Ankali 054
Lopuchová 58
www.anka.li
Antipearle 092
Janáčkovo nábřeží 61
T 703 333 206
www.antipearle.com
Art Restaurant Mánes 046
Masarykovo nábřeží 250/1
T 730 150 772
www.manesrestaurant.cz
Artisème 029
Velkopřevorské náměstí 4
T 776 493 169
www.artiseme.com
Atelier Pelcl 083
www.pelcl.cz
Augustine Spa 022
Augustine
Letenská 12/33
T 266 112 273
www.augustinehotel.com
(A)void Floating Gallery 074
Výtoň
T 602 211 181

B

Backyard 080
U Obecního dvora 2
T 605 894 096
www.back-yard.cz
Bajkazyl 074
Ke Sklárně 15
T 739 681 839
Bar Cobra 054
Milady Horákové 688/8
T 777 355 876
www.barcobra.cz

Bartida 010
Havelská 500/25
T 224 281 247
www.bartida-praha.cz
Bethlehem Chapel 028
Betlémské náměstí 255/4
T 224 248 595
www.bethlehemchapel.eu
Bistro Proti Proudu 045
Březinova 471/22
T 728 036 171
www.bistroprotiproudu.cz
Black Angel's 032
Staroměstské náměstí 29
T 224 213 807
www.blackangelsbar.cz
Bohemian Retro 080
Chvalova 8
T 607 914 992
www.bohemianretro.com
Bokovka 049
Dlouhá 37
T 731 492 046
www.bokovka.com
Monday to Friday, 5pm-1am;
Saturday, 3pm-1am
Book Therapy 095
Římská 35
T 223 009 949
www.booktherapy.cz

C

Café Jedna 026
Veletržní Palác
Dukelských hrdinů 47
T 778 440 877
www.cafejedna.cz

HOTELS

ADDRESSES AND ROOM RATES

Augustine 022
Room rates:
double, from €120;
Presidential Suite, from €2,340
Letenská 12/33
T 266 112 233
www.augustinehotel.com

Boho Hotel 018
Room rates:
double, from €170
Senovázná 1254/4
T 234 622 600
www.hotelbohoprague.com

Buddha-Bar Hotel 016
Room rates:
double, from €190
Jakubská 649/8
T 221 776 300
www.buddha-bar-hotel.cz

Carlo IV 017
Room rates:
double, from €130;
Junior Suite, from €210
Senovážné náměstí 13/991
T 224 593 111
www.dahotels.com/carlo-iv-prague

The Emblem 019
Room rates:
double, from €250;
Suite Library, from €800
Platnéřská 111/19
T 226 202 500
www.emblemprague.com

The Emerald 020
Room rates:
apartment, from €150;
Iwa, from €250
Žatecká 17/7
T 602 666 982
www.the-emerald-prague.com

Four Seasons 016
Room rates:
double, from €320
Veleslavínova 2a/1098
T 221 427 000
www.fourseasons.com

Hotel Ještěd 100
Room rates:
double, from €140
Horní Hanychov 153
Liberec
T 485 104 291
www.jested.cz

Hotel Josef 023
  Room rates:
  double, from €150;
  Room 801, €290
  Rybná 20
  T 221 700 901
  www.hoteljosef.com
Mandarin Oriental 030
  Room rates:
  double, from €230
  Nebovidská 459/1
  T 233 088 888
  www.mandarinoriental.com
Mezi Plůtky 102
  Room rates:
  double, from €160
  Čeladná 266
  Moravia
  T 606 924 232
  www.meziplutky.cz
Miss Sophie's New Town 016
  Room rates:
  double, from €70
  Melounova 3
  T 210 011 200
  www.miss-sophies.com

Port X 016
  Room rates:
  prices on request
  V Přístavu 4
  T 606 724 138
  www.portx.cz
Radisson Blu 016
  Room rates:
  double, from €130
  Žitná 561/8
  T 225 999 999
  www.radissonhotels.com
W 016
  Room rates:
  prices on request
  Václavské náměstí 826/25

WALLPAPER* CITY GUIDES

Executive Editor
Jeremy Case

Author
Joann Plockova

Art Editor
Jade R Arroyo

Editorial Assistant
Josh Lee

Photography Assistant
Freya Anderson

Photography Editor
Rebecca Moldenhauer

Contributors
Paul Sullivan
Evan Rail
Sean McGeady
Daniëlle Siobhán Mol
Emma Kalkhoven

Interns
Alex Merola
Hannah Makonnen

Prague Imprint
First published 2007
Sixth edition 2020

ISBN 978 1 83866 118 2

More City Guides
www.phaidon.com/travel

Follow us
@wallpaperguides

Contact
wcg@phaidon.com

Original Design
Loran Stosskopf

Map Illustrator
Russell Bell

Production Controller
Lily Rodgers

Wallpaper* Magazine
161 Marsh Wall
London E14 9AP
contact@wallpaper.com

Wallpaper*® is a
registered trademark
of TI Media

Phaidon Press Limited
Regent's Wharf
All Saints Street
London N1 9PA

Phaidon Press Inc
65 Bleecker Street
New York, NY 10012

All prices and venue
information are correct
at time of going to press,
but are subject to change.

A CIP Catalogue record for
this book is available from
the British Library.

PHOTOGRAPHERS

Aleš Jungmann
Stroj Času, p012
Carlo IV, p017
Boho Hotel, p018
The Emblem, p019
Hotel Josef, p023
Veletržní Palác, p026
Galerie Jaroslava
Fragnera, p028
Artisème, p029
Field, p031
Kro Kitchen, p033
Kuchyň, pp034-035
The Eatery, p036
Mazelab Coffee, p037
Moon Club, p038
SmetanaQ Café & Bistro,
p040
Kavárna Co Hledá Jméno,
p041
Dvojka, pp042-043
Le Valmont, p044
Bistro Proti Proudu, p045
Art Restaurant Mánes,
p046
Eska, p047
Bokovka, p048

Vinohradský Pivovar, p050
Meetfactory, p051
Nejen Bistro, p052
Lenka Míková, p055
Prague House of
Photography, p057
Kafka Sculpture, p061
CAMP, pp066-067
Museum Kampa, p068
Hrabalova Zeď,
pp070-071
National Museum New
Building, p076
Church of St Wenceslas,
p078, p079
Hana Zárubová, p081
Luciela Taschen, p082
100Class, pp084-085
Showroom, p086
Qubus Design Gallery,
p087
Naše Maso, p088
Chatty, p089
Cihelna, pp090-091
Antipearl, p092
Debut Gallery, p093
Book Therapy, p095

Sarah Blee
Jazz Dock, p053
Dox, p069
Villa Müller, p077

Boys Play Nice
Náplavka, p074, p075

Michal Czanderle
Hunt Kastner, pp062-063

Noshe
National Memorial,
pp010-011
Tower Park, p013
Nationale-Nederlanden
Building, pp014-015
House at the Black
Madonna, p027

David Zidlicky
Villa Tugendhat,
pp098-099

PRAGUE
A COLOUR-CODED GUIDE TO THE HOT 'HOODS

HRADČANY
Crowds flock to the rambling citadel; the charming hillside gardens are more tranquil

NOVÉ MĚSTO/VYŠEHRAD
The commercial hub buzzes with tourists and locals alike. A ruined castle lies to the south

MALÁ STRANA
Boasting cobbled streets and baroque palaces, this is period-drama Prague at its finest

JOSEFOV
Once the city's Jewish ghetto, the quarter has been colonised by high-fashion labels

ŽIŽKOV/VINOHRADY
Communist-era grit and bourgeois sophistication coexist in these residential areas

STARÉ MĚSTO
This tourist honeypot is worth a visit for Týn Church and the unique cubist architecture

For a full description of each neighbourhood, see the Introduction.
Featured venues are colour-coded, according to the district in which they are located.